G000041737

FAREWELL THOU BUSY WORLD

"Farewell, thou busy world! and may
We never meet again."
　　　—Charles Cotton to Isaak Walton

FAREWELL

THOU

BUSY

WORLD

John Hodgdon Bradley

THE DERRYDALE PRESS
LANHAM AND NEW YORK

THE DERRYDALE PRESS

Published in the United States of America
by The Derrydale Press
4720 Boston Way, Lanham, Maryland 20706

Distributed by NATIONAL BOOK NETWORK, INC.

Foreword copyright © 2000 by Fred Rice
First Derrydale edition 2000

Farewell Thou Busy World originally published in a limited edition by the Primavera Press, 1935.

The Derrydale Press edition contains several textual changes made by the author prior to his death that were not included in the 1935 edition.

Library of Congress Card Catalog Number: 00-030852

Bradley, John Hodgdon, 1898–
  Farewell thou busy world / John Hodgdon Bradley.
    p. cm.
  Contents: Escape—Friends of mine—Ten miles from Hollywood—Through the West in low—Mazourka Canyon—Concerning bait—A lake and a boy.
  ISBN 1-58667-013-1 (cloth : alk. paper)
  1. Natural history—West (U.S.) 2. Bradley, John Hodgdon, 1898– I. Title

QH104.5.W4 B73 2000
508.78—DC21   00-030852

To
Katharine

CONTENTS

FOREWORD

When I first encountered my grandfather, he was living on a hilltop overlooking the San Pasqual valley, a few miles from the town of Escondido, California. This was before Interstate 15 had pushed its way through, bringing the conveniences of commuter society to the largely rural area that surrounded the town and well before the San Diego zoo created a faux Serengeti in the valley below.

As I remember it, Escondido was a small town, not unlike the places immortalized in *Happy Days* or *American Graffiti*. But this was a long time before the nostalgia boom, when the fifties were just a calendar date and not a commodity or a marketing tool. It was also a time when wildness was still a possibility in southern California: Condors were breeding in the Los Padres National Forest, steelhead lived in the coastal streams, and wild salmon ran in the rivers of the Great Valley. It was even possible to imagine that somewhere, in a hidden corner of the Kings Canyon-Sequoia, there were vestigial populations of the golden bear, the California grizzly.

Of course, the full awareness of all nuances comes with age, if it comes at all. At the time, I was content to trace the wing patterns of birds from the Peterson guide and watch the hummingbirds squabble over position at the many feeders surrounding the house. I remember one gray morning when I discovered a toad in a depression under the large rock in the backyard and another time when my grandfather and I en-

1

countered a snake that stretched all the way across the road where we walked each afternoon.

Years later, I discovered that throughout his life my grandfather, John Bradley, had described similar encounters with the natural world through his articles in magazines and occasional writings. But by the time I made this discovery, I had already immersed myself in the seemingly endless environmental battles of the late 60's and early 70's. The federal government had already backed up the Colorado River into Glenn Canyon and was countenancing the same fate for the Grand Canyon down stream. The last redwoods on California's north coast were logged for patio decks and lawn furniture, most of California's few remaining free flowing rivers were dammed or threatened by dams, and development or destruction threatened wild lands throughout the West. So, when I came across this small book on a shelf in my parents' home, I was struck by the clarity of the voice and the unqualified support of wild creatures and wild places, wherever they are found. But clarity was not enough, and I spent years on myriad campaigns and causes before returning to these essays.

When I returned, I found in the essays something that separated them from most of the accounts I had poured over in my activist pursuits: For starters, there was almost no hyperbole. Coming from our lofty perch at the dawn of a new millennium, the absence of bells and whistles is quaint and old fashioned, a throwback to a time before modems and postmodern sensibilities. Uniformed by the large battles looming on the millennial horizon, these are essays that talk about wild spaces that lie adjacent to our homes and towns, at the edge of our gardens and outside the back door.

Our postmodern condition is one of extremes, hence our language is full of dire warnings and stern pronouncements. And, in the end, things do change—some. But while hyperbolic appeals to our reptilian brains are wonderful sources of flight-or-fight adrenaline rushes, they are hardly conducive to problem solving and reckoning with the sources of our difficulties. These essays remind us of that old virtue, patience, and to value watching and waiting. Would we be better off learning how to approach turtles in a pond than mastering *Tomb Raider*? Perhaps patience and watchfulness are not even in the realm of choices for most as they pursue the everyday busy-ness of their existence, but I believe that the encounters that my grandfather documents can still strike a cord as we rush about.

Telling all I know about the man who wrote these essays is relatively easy: We spent little time with my mother's father, usually around holidays or long weekends when we would visit him on his hilltop. I knew—or came to know—that he taught geography and paleontology at various colleges and universities, that he grew up in the Midwest and lived for a time in California, Montana, and Massachusetts before returning to California. Of course, I knew he was a writer and that he wrote textbooks. I also knew that he was a fisherman, a fly fisherman as it turned out, and I was told that he knew the famous Dan Bailey and perhaps some of the other legendary western fly fishermen.

There are bits of Bradley's biography embedded in these pieces: "Ten Miles From Hollywood" dates from the time he was teaching at USC, while "Through The West In Low" is probably the product of numerous cross country journeys from Massachusetts to Montana, where my mother and her family spent their summers. Other essays—"Friends Of Mine," "A Lake And A Boy" and parts of "Concerning Bait"—are reminiscences of a Midwest boyhood spent beside ponds, "mud lakes," and potholes. These are common places, local places, places that most of us can still encounter within a short distance of where we live.

The wild places described in these essays are largely accessible by anyone with eyes and ears. It is not necessary to mount a two-week expedition to recreate them. Still, my grandfather's account of that journey up Mazourka Canyon, a journey that is a study in patience and persistence, arrives at a place almost unimaginably beyond our everyday comprehension, to a time when ancient creatures inhabited a sea that covered the highest mountains. It is probably unnecessary to mention that every weekend, thousands of people stream by the mouth of Mazourka Canyon, oblivious to the story found in the rocks. In our quest for the wild and exotic, the extreme, we sometimes pass mileposts that are as significant as the thrills we seek. Is this a wild place, so close to a major highway, shopping mall, or factory?

4

I remember a trip I once took into the back country of the Sierra. I walked for nearly fifty miles from the west side of the range to a cluster of lakes in the shadow of Mt. Whitney, and I remember thinking that this was a remote spot, away from the crowds of people that flock to the mountain lakes in summer. And then, the next morning, I walked to the summit of Whitney and found the crowds who were working their way to the highest point in the contiguous forty-eight states. I looked down on the valley and saw the highway, the same highway my grandfather describes from his perch on top of Inyo Mountains, across the Owens Valley from the Sierra crest. For me, the illusion of wildness was dispelled when I reached the summit. In retrospect, I think I may have deprived myself of fully experiencing the sun and wind on bare granite, the marmots in the talus, and the reflection of mountain peaks in the clear lake waters. I missed these things because my definition of the experience required it to contain something that wasn't there, something that conformed to my preconceived notion about wildness and wilderness that I could not find in my relatively cursory inventory of the situation.

Is this a wild place? In the extreme definition, driven by our search for adrenaline rushes, maybe the relatively ordinary is not. But if we are looking for ways to reconnect with our simpler, more primitive nature, even the relatively ordinary experience provides us with an opportunity to experience that bond with the wild world, to listen to the wind and water, and to slow the pace of our daily life.

These essays were written more than sixty-five years ago, long before much of our modern sensibility about wilderness and wild places took form. Since that time, the world has changed some. There is now a system of wilderness areas that embraces the Mazourka Canyon and extends out from the edges of Glacier Park and Yellowstone. Community planners have added "open space" and green belts to their arsenal of tools to preserve and protect the wild things at the edges of our cities and towns. Congress has enacted legislation to protect our air and water, and the Endangered Species Act affords a certain modicum of protection for some, though not all, of the wild things that human agency has placed in danger of extinction.

Opinion polls continue to show broad support for measures that secure and enhance environmental safeguards. Yet, arguably, wild places are in greater jeopardy now than they were half a century ago. Does this mean that we should increase our efforts in the areas that have shown only incremental success in the past? Do we really need more designated wilderness, stronger environmental protection laws, more stringent safeguards to protect critical habitat? Probably so, but the questions raised by these essays are also worthy of our consideration: Is preservation enough, or is it also necessary to "sedulously avoid every serious concern of man," to move "away from turmoil" towards "the fruitless babble of mountain streams" and "the runaway experiences on the other side of the world where animals live?" Do we need to take time out from the all-encompassing busy-ness to experience our immediate surroundings? I believe the questions raised in *Farewell Thou Busy World* are as important today as they were when they were first written.

Fred Rice
Missoula-Helena
February-March 2000

ESCAPE

Sooner or later most men find themselves groaning under the weight of civilization; yearning to escape the ambitions, obligations, and repressions of human society. They find themselves searching for something that was lost when their ancestors abandoned the wilderness to the animals. When opportunity comes they instinctively return to their homeland of an eon ago, and in an animal's world seek the peace their own world withholds.

These pages record the simple adventures of one who has yielded to the call of the wilderness. They sedulously avoid every serious concern of man. They deal with runaway experiences on the other side of the world where the animals live; with time stolen from customary pursuits; with the fruitless babble of mountain streams and the idle thoughts of people who love them. They attempt neither to instruct nor to excite; but rather to lead the reader away from turmoil, of which just possibly he has had enough. Those who see chiefly mosquitoes in the woods, dirt in the desert, and dampness at sea had better turn away. They would not understand.

FRIENDS OF MINE

Not least among a sportsman's joys are memories
that come on winter evenings, when smoke is rising from his pipe, and a log sputters in the fire-
place. At such a time the true hunter tastes again
the triumph of an antlered head brought low; the
true fisherman feels again the weight of bulging
creel. Alas, such joys are not for me. When fish
sulked and ducks flew out of range, I have rested
on my oars, and shared the laughter of the loon.
And so I remember best the shameful hours when
my gun was resting against a tree, and I was
throwing crumbs to hungry squirrels.

I think it all began many years ago when I got
acquainted with a snake. Perhaps that snake was
the beginning of my failure as a sportsman. Be-

11

fore she came into my life, I was ruled by a single passion—to lure black bass from a little lake in Illinois. Men from the city had fished too well, and bass were scarce. But the faith that moves a mud scow along five miles of shoreline when fish are not biting, must produce something in the end. For me it produced a ritual, born of failure and nourished by regrets. Among other things I had learned that honest finny flesh with a live wiggle was more convincing than a wooden minnow with all the endowments of art. I knew that a race of giant minnows haunted the weed beds far from the lesser tribes of the shallows. An old Englishman had told me how to catch them and how to bait them for bass. A piece of liver and a handful of bran were placed in a tin can in the sunlight. After a few days the liver became fly-blown, maggots grew and fattened in the bran. Another day saw them creamy in color and firm enough for a fish hook. Shiners could not resist them.

Before the sun had cleared the treetops, and the lake was hot glass ruddy with dawn and smoking with mist, we would glide to the edge of the weed beds, peering through the fog for the play of shiners. Bluegills in a feeding school slap the water but shiners are silver blades that cut cleanly and almost without noise. A school would be sighted and cracker crumbs tossed about to keep it near the boat. The shiners were caught on tiny hooks baited with maggots and hung on a crow quill to sense the Lilliputian nibbles. Two dozen shiners might be in the bait can before breakfast, shiners as long as one's hand and as brilliant as sun on water. Even when all other methods failed, bass could be taken with these by slow trolling along the edge of the weed beds.

It was while breeding maggots that I met the snake. Garter snakes lived in the swamps on the west shore of our lake. With other boys I had often gone there to kill and to boast of the tally afterwards. When a boy sighted a snake he would run to it and place a firm heel below the reptile's head. Grasping the snake by the tail, he would break the victim's back by that same quick motion of the wrist used in snapping towels at each other after swimming. One day I found a large garter snake pilfering my liver can on the dump heap behind the hotel. Perhaps this was the first time that curiosity quieted the killer in me. I had never seen a serpent at table before. Next day the snake was in my liver can again. This time I caught her and put her in a cracker box covered with chicken wire.

She charmed us with her strange ways. Gophers, field mice, frogs, toads, flies were lavished upon her. These she refused or accepted demurely, almost reluctantly. She ate one large green frog every three days. We remembered our own appetites and marveled at hers. When at last she grabbed a frog, we stood around for hours, held by the fascination of the meal traveling slowly down her long body. She gradually became accustomed to us and would pick flies from our fingers and let us handle her. But she languished in spite of our devotion, perhaps because of it, and died in less than a month.

Then followed a craze for small garter snakes. We knew a field where the little chaps were plentiful. I managed to catch eight of them, each one about six inches long and no thicker than a pencil. A few had recently sloughed their skins and were beautifully marked. Every morning I found two or three of them, freed in some mysterious way, lying under their prison box. They never tried to escape farther. If these snakes did not become friendly, they at least grew accustomed to me. They learned to eat from my hand and to sit in my shirt pocket, darting their forked tongues and flashing their beady eyes at strangers. One, more accomplished than the others, could hang by his jaws on my finger. They all died before their time, no doubt from overhandling. Somehow this experience modified my loathing for snakes. Since then I have let the harmless ones go free.

I think it was the same summer that turtles began to interest me. Ordinarily these creatures are more warming as soup than as comrades. Perhaps because of their very deficiencies we boys grew fond of them. We sought them in a weed-choked channel that linked our lake to another. Turtles of many styles and sizes plied their business in the dense water grasses. We went to the hunt on rare summer mornings when the south wind held her breath. On such days the weeds near the inlet poked their heads above the water, and so did the turtles. We learned to distinguish weeds from heads, and to choose quickly the head of greatest promise. Then the boy at the oars would push the lithe duck boat slowly and silently nearer. At the proper moment the boy in the bow would slip over the gunwale into the tangled growth. Slowly he would work his way, chest deep in ooze, partly crawling, partly swimming toward the quarry. Sometimes the head would stay above water until the amphibious Nimrod was within five feet. Then with a forward movement, he would bring his body flush with the surface of the water and pounce upon the unsuspecting reptile.

15

Adventure lurked in the sedges of our turtle grounds. A slimy live thing would sometimes squeeze from under our intruding feet. Water snakes, whom we distrusted as poisonous, would sometimes squirm our way. Most of the turtles were of the "soft shell" and "mud" varieties. One day the knotty head of a large "snapper" was sighted. We approached in the usual manner, but discreetly used a small fishing net for the final bag. In the boat the monster escaped the meshes and ran up and down deck, snapping viciously at our bare toes. Now it is well known among boys that a snapping turtle holds tightly to a good thing when he finds it, and holds on as long as life is in him. We got that turtle out of the boat as fast as we could.

A derelict scow furnished an aquarium for our captives. We garnished it with the comforts so dear to the indolent soul of a turtle. There our pets would sit all day long, just blinking and looking with professorial calm. We prized the small ones because they were more difficult to find. Bunt caught one that could hide under a quarter. I remember making the experiment with a quarter earned by selling frogs to an itinerant fisherman. Bunt was envied by all the boys along two miles of lake shore, until he killed his pet with devotion.

But turtles at best were unsatisfactory friends. Their sluggish natures responded only to flies. When Fatty got an air rifle we set all our young turtles free and devoted our best efforts to shooting their parents off logs along shore. It may be that one of my erstwhile pets will escape accidental death. If he does, I know he will still be blinking at the sun when my children's grandchildren are burned out, and in all those years he will never have loved and never have hated, and never have longed for a high powered automobile.

I did not realize it at the time, but my decline as a fisherman was well along several years ago, when I played with the minnows in a lake back in the North Country. I should have been seining them for bait, but instead I lay for hours on the warm sand with my feet in the water, while the small fry gathered about, nosing and nibbling my toes. Emerson made much of the fact that Thoreau caught fishes in his hands, but Emerson did not know how easy it is to gain the confidence of a fish. Before the afternoon was over my companions in Blue Lake ate bread crumbs from my fingers, and swam into my cupped hand without fear.

On another occasion, paddling a canoe near the shore of an Adirondack lake, I discovered a family of horned pout. There under the edge of a bog was the fat black head of God's ugliest creature, looking at me through yellow bead-like eyes. On the next day two of the fish were under the bog. At first they disappeared in the mud when I approached too close. Slowly their fear left them until I could come within a few feet. I am sure that if I had remained long enough to learn their language, they, too, would have eaten from my hand.

Birds, likewise, can be approached. Many of the bolder ones of orchard, woodlot, and meadow will make the first advance. The chickadee, the titmouse, the junco, and the nuthatch draw away from grey skies and driven snow to the warm odors of the farmyard. They have been tamed. Wrens, martins, robins, jays, woodpeckers may even take certain familiarities. The camp robber, with the soul of a mosquito, will surely pester the human who ventures far into the woods.

Hunted birds are the wariest. Only once have I succeeded in quieting the fear of a wild duck. I was camped on a cove off the northeastern end of Lake Champlain. Each morning at daybreak a female mallard came to the water in front of my tent and quacked at me. She was apparently defying my trespass upon ground sacred to ducks. A man may be awake at five in the morning, but his sympathies aren't. I disliked that duck. Her alarm broke through the mist each morning at the same time. Despairing of sleep, I tried to imitate her with a quack of my own. I must have interested her because after a few days she seemed to wait for my quacks before continuing hers. Her curiosity at last drove her out of the water to my tent, no doubt to learn the source of such depraved quacking. I heard the quacks approach, and saw an inquiring beak. Slowly a duck's head appeared between the flaps. I threw her a raisin which she ate. For several mornings she answered my quacks and came for raisins. One day she failed to come. Days grew into weeks until I began to fear for my duck. But she was quite all right. She sailed by the cove one afternoon, head erect and beak pointing stiffly ahead, eight ducklings in the offing. Only the trees across the bay answered my call with a feeble, unimpassioned quack. It hurts to be jilted.

I once had a similar experience with a marmot. Furred animals are more amenable to kindness than reptiles, birds, and fishes, perhaps because of their higher intelligence. They run away because they see us as death. But they respond almost instinctively to friendly advances. In our national parks bears, deer, elk, and ground squirrels in their fondness for peanuts and candy become fearless nuisances. One summer when I was hiking with a companion over the high trails of Glacier Park, I had a similar experience with a marmot. On the rocky summit of Piegan Pass we stopped to eat lunch, tired from the climb, wearied with peaks and sunlit distances. Gradually we became conscious of our immediate surroundings. Frost blasted shale was everywhere, and scarcely a blade of any growing plant. The subterranean homes of that mountaineering woodchuck, the marmot, tunneled the rocks in many places. We had been seated but a short time when a large marmot poked his head from a den not thirty feet below us, and whistled shrilly in our direction. Now of all the more plentiful animals in the park, the marmot is the most fearful of man. We were surprised when he ate the food tossed to him and when he came slowly toward us for more. Quite unabashed he joined us and chewed on an old glove, salty with perspiration. He let us pet him. I have told this story to seasoned Park guides. They listened courteously.

A man meets with odd things in the woods. The wood thrush is a friendly bird in the South, where he enters towns and vies with robins on lawns. Farther north and west he shrinks into the deep woods. I once found the home of a wood thrush in a thicket on a western river. Spring was young and it was nesting time. The beauty of an April day was being born again. The ground was damp with dew and birds were active. A dove was sobbing somewhere in the distance, while nearby a little wren was noisily jubilant. A towhee was pecking in the brush.

My attention was arrested by the nervous antics of a male wood thrush. He was trying to lure me away from the nest but I knew his game. I found the nest hidden in the branches of a bush not far from the ground. The mother thrush was sitting. I moved toward her with the caution that all bird lovers learn, so quietly and slowly that I might almost have been the stump of a tree. She watched my approach with fear in her eyes, but not until I was within three feet did she join her mate in a nearby tree. Both hurled anathemas at me while I investigated the contents of the nest. I found two thrush eggs and the larger egg of a cowbird. I removed the parasite and retreated. Perhaps the favor was not appreciated, but on the next day when I approached, the mother thrush did not seem to fear me. At the time I could imagine she welcomed me, she let me come so very near.

I came back several mornings. One day I saw that something was wrong. Little rhythmic quivers ran through her spread wings. Slowly I drew nearer, nearer than I had ever been before. I stretched my arm toward her, so slowly that the muscles ached, and with a trembling hand, lifted her from the nest. I found her trouble a new egg that refused to join the others in the nest. I had to work a little to remove it, but she made no struggle. Her mate, who did not understand, tried to raise his courage to peck me.

I watched the nest until all the young birds had left. The mother thrush accepted me as no other wild bird ever has. She took food for her family and for herself, and would almost never fly from her perch on the edge of the nest when I came near. I have my doubts about many things, but I believe this bird and I were friends.

Of course, wild animals must struggle to live, and empty stomachs do not make full hearts. Wiser heads than mine can vouch for the relentless push of life. Sadder hearts than mine will deny any friendliness in nature. But a man sees some odd things in the woods. Oddest of all, perhaps, is the animal who kills for hate or for fun, who walks erect and speaks a foreign language.

TEN MILES FROM HOLLYWOOD

For no particular reason he came to have the name of Adolph. It is unusual that a lizard should have a name at all in a land where his tribe must number millions; that the name should imply, by however remote a connotation, the nature of a wolf is both ridiculous and unjust. But such is the illogic of the human mind. Adolph's temperament is benign, and when there are no ants about he lives a blameless life in his little corner of the world.

His home is a chink in the rock wall of the stairway that leads from the house to the garage. Of all the wild creatures whose domain we invaded when we came to live in the canyon, Adolph appears least suspicious of our basic integrity. We like him because he flatters us. He lets us sit down beside him on his favorite rock and runs away only when we try to touch him.

He eats the insect tidbits we offer him, cautiously but without cringing. There is no reason to fear us and Adolph seems to know it. His is the speed of light when his sensitive nerves detect a threat. Even when lying on his belly in the sun with limbs stretched limply behind him, his little yellow-rimmed eyes become suddenly alert when we approach. They observe us with mild distrust and at the same time slyly suggest that although our heads may be wondrously fashioned, our muscles are clumsy absurdities which even a napping lizard may disdain.

I suppose it is heresy in this day of science to think of Adolph as anything more than a bundle of reflexes and tropisms. Adolph may indeed be very automatic, and perhaps he responds not at all to the spirit with which we bring him flies. But he responds to the flies and in that regard at least is not unlike our nobler selves. I have watched him for months and I am forced to believe that, howsoever aged and impersonal may be the impulses that direct his actions, they give Adolph a personality as authentic in its way as our own.

When he cocks his head like a bird (with

whom, we are told, he shares his remoter ancestry) to inspect you with supercilious but scrutinizing hauteur, you can scarcely escape the feeling of being judged a bit hypercritically by a person of importance. Adolph is only eight inches long and more than half of him is tail, but his dignity is dinosaurian. Whether looking out at the world with stiffly elevated front or darting lightly from rock to rock, he seems never to forget that he is handsome. Adolph, I fear, is a poseur and shallow at heart, but I like him because he pays me the compliment of not being afraid of me.

The fact that Adolph is the scion of a noble race may explain, if it fails to excuse, his obvious self-satisfaction. His forbears once ruled the earth. Though time has diluted it, blood of the Mesozoic overlords is in his veins. And when the masters of those far off days went down to oblivion, Adolph's more immediate ancestors found a way of escape. Merely to endure so long amid the stern exigencies of the world is an accomplishment. Scientists say that Adolph's race is far from intelligent, and it may be that Adolph knows nothing of his nobility. Perhaps it is just as well. As an instinctive aristocrat he is charming.

When an ant lucklessly happens by, murder

rises in Adolph's soul. He simply cannot resist ants. But never was murder consummated with finer delicacy. Adolph cocks his head, blinks the dust from his eyes, runs lightly toward the victim and flicks it into his mouth with an invisibly rapid stab of the tongue. The act is graceful, bloodless, instantaneous, and utterly nonchalant. One day a blundering colony of ants settled not far from Adolph's solarium. He might easily have stood over the swarm and in five minutes made an end of it. But Adolph is no gourmand. At respectable intervals he approached the colony, flicked up an ant, and then returned to his favorite rock. He never hurried and he never took more than one ant at a time. In this fashion the feast was prolonged for two days, and I sincerely hope the delight of it was as exquisite as it seemed.

When we first came to the canyon Adolph was but one of many lizards who haunted the chinks in the garden walls. Now he is one of the few who remain. I have not been willing to believe our presence so detestable to lizards that they must abandon the premises. I have felt rather that it must be the dog. More recently I decided that Patsy's enthusiastic but ineffectual sallies were not the true explanation for the disappearance of the lizards.

Snakes are the hereditary enemies of lizards. When a beautiful snake all ringed with red, black, and yellow was seen near the entrance to the garage, it did not immediately occur to me that here might well be the decimator of the lizards . I was more interested in ascertaining from imperfect observations whether the yellow rings were bordered on each side by the black or whether the black rings were bordered by the yellow. My interest was not entirely academic. Snakes with the former pattern are harmless, whereas those with the latter secrete a venom more powerful than that of the rattlesnake. Unhappily my informants remembered only that the snake was the most beautiful they had ever seen.

Two months later I was called from my study by Patsy's excited barking. Squirming before her on the cement stairway not ten feet from Adolph's home was the banded snake. Before it wriggled into a crevice, I recognized the markings of the ringed king snake, a harmless "mimic" of the deadly coral snake. Harmless, that is, to men, because it lacks fangs and venom; but death to lizards, whose agility it equals and whose strength it greatly exceeds. It suddenly occurred to me that life is not all posing for such as Adolph. Who knows but that this very instant Adolph himself may not be caught in those cruel coils in some dark recess of my garden wall. I have tried to reach that snake but he is more clever than I. Yet Adolph is also clever. May his good luck hold, for he is really a charming fellow.

Adolph has done more than amuse me and I am grateful. He has made me curious about my animal neighbors from whom I am learning many things. He has taught me that there is more in this canyon than an evening retreat from a confused and tired world. This mountain world, which had been but the background for a mood, was in reality a theatre alive with drama. Although only ten miles from Hollywood, the canyon portals abruptly separate the world that men have made from the world that men have rather generally forgotten. Within, some magic dissolves the sucking drone of rubber on concrete into the twitter of bush-tits. The obvious geometry of streets and houses melts into the intricate, subtle, and satisfying lines of mountain slopes. Colors become scattered and elusive; the stench of half-burned gasoline yields to the odors of earth. Here in a jumble of peaks, only the foxes and coyotes howl at night, and no murmur of human blatancy ever stirs the air. This canyon is really only an insignificant mark in a vast picture, but it is a genuine fragment of the dwindling domain that men have left alone.

In winter when rain drizzles and mist thickens the air, the pygmy forests of chaparral on southern California's coast ranges assume the aspect so dear to a northerner's heart. For a short while they seem lush and deep and green. But the sun soon dispels the illusion, and dry brown deadness returns. Thanks to Adolph, I now know that the deadness lies more in the unseeing eye than on the slopes of this nearly desert canyon. Watching him I began also to see something of the world he inhabits, something of the drama that throbs amid these rocks and thorns.

For a long time I had been aware of the birds, but they were not the birds I loved. They only made me dream at times of old friends beyond the Rockies. There were no birds half so friendly as robins here, no thrushes to sing one on a summer evening into ecstasy. Even the dimly familiar ones seemed somehow strange and distant.

Against one bird in this canyon, however, no indifference may stand. It is impossible to sit for an hour in the garden without a brush with him. The brush may be too nearly literal for comfort. There comes a sudden whirring, a stir in the air beside your ear; and a feathered bullet, which you recognize as a hummingbird, flashes by.

Hummingbirds are beautiful, but your first thought may well not be of beauty. A slight error by whatever it is that motivates these living projectiles and a needle might have punctured your brain.

Fortunately hummingbirds do not err. There are times when a man believes he has seen an embodiment of perfection. A mountain goat weaving up a vertical cliff like a fly on a wall, an antelope racing with the wind on an upland mesa, a porpoise cutting the waves with no visible exertion—each in its way approaches locomotive perfection. The hummingbird achieves it. Whether hanging in the air motionless but for the nearly invisible beating of wings, or shifting from flower to flower in a tireless probing after nectar; whether flying forward like a streak of metallic green light or darting to either side, up or down, or even backwards—the hummingbird is as perfect a machine as this world affords.

At mating time these little engines fill the canyon with whirring. It is not unusual to see a male in violent pursuit of a female, the latter flying swiftly backward and staying her lover's ardor as best she may with her stiletto bill. That she does not always escape is attested by the scores of baby hummers now in the tobacco trees about the house. These young birds are fearlessly curious of man. They hang in the air for seconds a few inches from your face or repeatedly dart by, swerving just enough to avoid collision.

I have often tried to imagine what goes on in their tiny heads and I have concluded, not without regret, that although their flight is perfect and their bodies trim and lovely, their souls may be of lesser excellence. So similar are the manifestations of hate and love that it is not always easy to decide whether they are quarreling or courting. But it is certain that, whatever the reason, they are continually disturbing one another. I fear they are both irritable and meddlesome.

They not only drive individuals of their own kind from favorite feeding grounds, but they frequently intrude upon birds of different feather for no obvious reason except an urge to be disagreeable. The western flycatcher is a diffident and well-mannered bird. He carefully chooses a perch from which he may launch into the air after passing insects. He makes his living without poaching on the preserves of any other bird. I suspect his life would be reasonably happy but for the hummingbirds. They see him on his perch and bedevil him with their bills until the poor embarrassed chap moves on.

It may be that in the world of birds too, all is not gold that glitters. The hummingbird is the

31

darling of our guests because he is small and showy. But I believe him likewise cantankerous, cold, and self-centered, our most intriguing and ungenerous neighbor. Undeflected by the softer feelings he flashes brilliantly through life, but not quite brilliantly enough to conceal the stain of iron which holds his beauty somewhat short of the ultimate.

Once an interest awakens, one is continually amazed that these barren-looking coast ranges should hold so many birds. More numerous even than the hummingbirds are the linnets. Almost alone among native birds, the linnet has held his ground against the tidal wave of English sparrows that rolled over America from the east. In California one does see an occasional English sparrow about freight yards, stock pens, and on the cornices of buildings; but in the country the linnet is still king. These little reddish birds are everywhere, chattering about the houses, resting on the telephone wires, gathering seeds along the mountain sides. Because they are always cheerful I can forgive them their annual depredation in my fruit trees. They simply know that life is sweet, and it is worth a few apricots to hear them say so.

Bush-tits, too, are legion. They drift in little grey clouds through the sycamores and live oaks about the house. One never sees nor thinks of bush-tits singly. Their personality exists only in the aggregate. They are but wisps of animation searching restlessly but hopefully through the barrens of the world.

Early in the morning before the sun has sapped the fresh vigor of day, I sometimes sit on the mountainside and watch the pageant of the birds. The wrens, like wrens the earth around, are bursting with vitality. A brood has just been hatched in a ventilator tile in the side of the house and the parents are busily gathering insects to cram into the insatiable maws of their babies. They cease chattering and flicking their tails only to sing. And such a song! As an expression of sheer high spirits it has no equal. Its enthusiasm is contagious, and while I listen to it in the cool of the morning I am not much moved by scientific scepticism which insists that wrens are not the happy little creatures they appear.

Then there is the wren-tit, voice of the chaparral. His song, a single repeated staccato note ending in rapid acceleration, rings through the still air while the bird remains hidden in the brush. Something a little plaintive in the tone suggests that even birds must sometime buttress courage with a song. Other denizens of the brush scratch a living more stolidly. The brown towhee is a peasant who seldom lifts his head to sing. The thrasher is obviously too proud of his long curved bill to suffer disturbing thoughts. Each follows the channel of his own destiny through the undergrowth at my feet.

Higher are birds of other temperaments. The black-headed grosbeak feeds on the ground but rises in the air with the buoyancy of song. I wonder if he can sense the sweetness of his melody. I wonder if the hooded orioles that shame the flowers can know how beautiful they are. I wonder if the kingbird who is driving a hawk over the mountain can feel the surge of that conflict which is life wherever life may wander.

One by one they pass, in a moving picture which is not so much a hodge-podge of creatures with fascinating ways as an epitome of life itself. All of life's varied display, perhaps all of life's meaning is here in this canyon. Sometimes a coyote, whose home is the wasteland beyond the rim of peaks, ventures toward the house. Not long ago a scrawny pair came over to meet my dog. For a golden half hour of respite they romped with her on the hillside, forgetting for the time both hunger and the animosity of men.

So close is the wilderness that even the foxes sometimes come into the yard and nibble the shrubs. Usually they are unobtrusive neighbors whom we seldom see though a family of them lives in a hole not a stone's throw from the house. Only the excitement of love disturbs their cautious quietness. Under its compulsion they howl with a strange noise that starts like the barking of a dog and ends like the crowing of a rooster. But now they are quiet again, and baby foxes can be seen in the draw above the oaks.

Howsoever much we may see ourselves in the personalities of wild animals, howsoever clearly we may perceive in their daily struggle to live the unremitting conflict of our own existence, in our hearts we remain fundamentally aloof from the rest of nature. With the self-satisfaction that distinguishes men from the rest of creatures, we either entirely disregard our humbler brethren or we play god to them. But on such a rare occasion as when a man finds himself between a grizzly bear and her cubs, he realizes that he is not yet entirely a law unto himself. There are no longer any grizzlies in these mountains, but the rattlesnakes well serve the same chastening purpose. In a world where nearly all animals must quake at the approach of the two-legged tyrant, the rattlesnake turns the tables and makes the tyrant quake. God may have made rattlesnakes for some other, but certainly for no worthier, reason.

Like certain other weary sojourners, the rattlesnake has found life sweetest in the sunshine of southern California. Everywhere men hate him, both because he goes on his belly through the grass, and because he protects his life with a deadly poison. They have all but exterminated him throughout most of his natural range. But in the semi-arid mountains of California and Mexico, on land that few men traverse and no man desires to own, the rattlesnake yet thrives. Ten of the thirteen species of North American rattlesnakes still inhabit these regions.

Recently a diamond rattler over four feet long wandered towards the house, no doubt for the innocent purpose of drinking at the patio pool. We met near the woodpile. Immediately the snake threw himself into the familiar coiled attitude of defense. One of the most ominous sounds in nature emanated from the end of his vibrating tail. The coils of his body remained frozen but his heart-shaped head moved with my every movement. Such are the temperaments of men and rattlesnakes that when the two meet, one must die. I retreated to look for a weapon. The snake relaxed but made no attempt to escape. His body was nearly as thick as my forearm.

Failing to find a club of safe length, I picked up a log from the woodpile. Again the snake coiled and rattled defiance. He was sullen, threatening, terrible; but beneath my loathing was admiration for an animal who chose rather to look death squarely in the eye than to run away.

The first log partly paralyzed the lower part of his body. He could yet have made the cover of the nearby mountain slope, but instead he painfully, resolutely, coiled again. Nine logs battered his body before that fearful, fearless head lay still.

Another rattlesnake had capitulated to the whim of fate that granted to man alone the ability to throw a missile; an ability which renders impotent the strongest teeth and claws, the deadliest fangs and the surest muscles in the animal world. I buried him with mixed feelings. Within the limits set upon him, he too had been an excellent hunter. And this at least may doubtless be said for him: that he never knew fear; that he killed only for hunger or defense; that he never tracked a helpless deer through the woods merely for the joy of seeing it die.

At night when the crickets are awake and the hylas are croaking the song which only a hyla may enjoy, another voice comes out of the darkness, the voice of the poorwill. But it is more symbol than sound, for in the tone is all the sweetness and the sadness and the braveness of life itself. "Your day is done," it seems to say, "my night is just beginning. Everywhere, always, life must be about its business: struggling but never quite succeeding, suffering but never quite succumbing, reveling but never quite forgetting, going but never quite arriving. A hard, a joyous, an endless business. Poorwill! Poorwill!"

THROUGH THE WEST IN LOW

Some love the West romantically. These are generally Easterners who thrill to its charms in the summer months on the porch of the El Tovar, on the corral fence of Eaton's ranch, and along the horse trails of our national parks. When winter creeps out of the mountain passes and railroad rates relax into comfortable round-trip fares, the romantic crusade pours toward the setting sun. Forest fires, drought, and the depression are powerless to stem the flood, for behind it is the drive of the human spirit to be free, and freedom is imagined to lie just beyond the customary horizon. Fords and chauffeured limousines, day coaches and compartment Pullmans penetrate to every corner of the West, scattering

39

school teachers and business executives, debutantes and dowagers over a million square miles of wilderness.

Some invite their souls a little timidly as they skirt the Shoshone abyss atop a yellow bus, shuddering at the turnouts, marveling with pounding heart at the canyon and the dam, fingering the more expensive curios at Buffalo Bill's lodge before buying a postcard. There is never any doubt that they have come from regions where the crude vigor of rock and forest and mountain air does not exist. Others tog themselves in ten gallon hats, flannel shirts, whipcord trousers, and high boots. They grip your hand until you wince. These are the instantaneous Westerners, Hollywood's gift to the open spaces.

Only a few are of the blasé breed who have been everywhere and have seen everything, and are mildly disappointed in Man and God. Most prefer to think of the West as big, beautiful, but above all, romantic. They listen to the yarning of the guides, enthralled by the description of places that do not exist and events that never happened.

Romantic gullibility is not the sole trait that unifies the westward pilgrimage. Hurry, nervous offspring of our times, is always along. Whether it be to sit on the brink of the Grand Canyon drinking in the sublimities, or marveling that here in all the world one can spit a mile, what is done must be done quickly, for the bus leaves in half an hour. A ride over Teddy's trail in the Bad Lands, the sight of a mountain goat in Glacier and a geyser in Yellowstone, a toboggan slide in summer on the flanks of Rainier, a roller-coaster dash through the redwoods, the firefall at Yosemite, a beach and a movie studio in Los Angeles, an Indian in a sheet at Santa Fé—then home again to Springfield in thirty days. For forty days, Alaska may be thrown in; and for sixty both Alaska and the Hawaiian Islands. Those who yearn further may return via Hongkong in four months.

We who spend much of our lives in the West are just as great an enigma to the annual pilgrims as they are to us. For however much they may flatter the great open spaces, they use the opening to escape when autumn comes round. Their judgment is almost unanimous: the West is a wonderful place to see but not to inhabit. Perhaps the movement that boomerangs their bodies out and back applies also to their minds. At any rate they are gone when the geese come honking down the Rockies from Canada.

Eastern friends who have followed me into the heart of a lonely mountain range, whose enthusiasm was high when rainbows were rising to the fly, and not completely withered when saddles bred woe and nights were frosty, wonder why anyone should choose the West as a permanent home. "God's country" becomes "the sticks," a God-forsaken wilderness, when they think of staying in it forever. Yet most bonafide Westerners are transplanted Easterners, who in some mysterious and miraculous way escaped the tyranny of the post-validation end of a railroad ticket. They are typically people who have consciously chosen the setting for their lives. Not many are able to make such a choice, and of these not many choose the West. Gophers are still the chief inhabitants of the hinterland. But when you find a man between the Dakotas and the Coast Ranges whom the flurries of autumn do not drive to the railroad station, you have most likely found a man who lives where he does because he wants to. And when the last tourist disappears beyond the eastern horizon, plenty of dust but few envious glances follow him.

Many Westerners love the West, knowing that it is neither so good nor so bad as it might be. The snapshot impressions of schedule-enslaved tourists, whether good or bad, are usually overcolored. Most visitors interpret the new West in terms of their conception of the old, and succeed only in misunderstanding both.

Much of the charm of the traditional West lay in its wildness, its wooliness, and its hospitality. Railroads, towns, farms, and mines have driven the wildness to the remoter mountains. The Indian is on his reservation, the bison in his grave, the road agent in the city; and with these have passed the snarliest kinks in the wooliness. As for hospitality, it exists in the West, here and there, just as it exists in other localities. Western people are perhaps less conventional in their relations with one another, but not necessarily more hospitable. The West is still richer in acres than in men. Its people have known isolation and have learned self-sufficiency. The social graces which grow in settled communities languish at the frontier where the fight against Nature is hard. And too, the homesteader and the rancher have so often been swindled by the stranger that they no longer welcome him with open heart, however much that heart may be longing for human companionship. Cattle and sheep have proved safer comrades.

Then there is the tradition of opportunity. The West has been the El Dorado of young romantics, middle-aged bankrupts, and elderly dyspeptics; and with good reason, for in the past it has yielded a rich harvest of adventure, fortune, and health. But today the railroads are built, the range is all but gone, the desirable free lands have been homesteaded. The timber is owned by great lumber companies or protected in national forests. The richest mines have been discovered and are controlled by New York capitalists. The major irrigation and power projects are preempted by the government and the public utilities. In a land of hot winds and little rain, dry farming is a very unromantic and unprofitable business. Farming on irrigated land is like farming in regions of sufficient rainfall, except that water carried through ditches is expensive, markets are more distant, but crops are not noticeably more lucrative. Nevada's desperate attempt to control the divorce market is sad proof of how her resources have failed her, Nevada whose boundaries enclose some of the richest silver deposits in the world. The West of the Anacoda Copper Mining Company and Boulder Dam is not the West of the covered wagon and J. J. Hill. Its romance is harder to discover, its fortunes elude the individual. Health is the sole ingredient of the old tradition that survives. Western climate has resisted both time and the market crash.

To live in the West is not only to reduce the scale of one's material ambitions but to put up with downright annoyances. The heart of the

West is a long day from the Pacific Coast, twice as far from Chicago, three times as far from the Atlantic seaboard. Few Westerners, however enthusiastic, have severed the sentimental ties which bind them to the land and to the people of their youth. Travel is a periodic necessity and an expensive one. Freight rates are high and living is costly where many of the essentials must be imported. Freight rates, indeed, are leeches that have thriven so well in the thin western soil that they may occasionally attach themselves to a homegrown product. Crude oil, for example, may be selling for thirty cents a barrel not two hundred miles away, but gasoline seldom strays far from the vicinity of thirty cents a gallon. Beef is seldom exposed to the weakening influence of corn, and its consumption is more often a necessity than a pleasure. Music may penetrate even to western Colorado (usually via the ether which, like the country, is rough); but it often comes canned and smelling of the tin. Drab little sunbaked towns and their people give off the essence of sagebrush more strongly than culture. "Why," said a legislator when more books were requested for the library of a western state university, "I'll bet not one of your professors has read all the books you have there now!"

The satisfactions of western life are less easily

catalogued—yet they certainly exist, both for the resident and for the visitor. Unfortunately the resident must take the bad with the good. The visitor, who may indulge the good without the bad, does not generally take time to do so.

The machine civilization, which leads men in crowded urban communities to all the well-known palliatives for too much work or too much leisure, has only begun to affect the West. Not that Westerners are very different from other people, but that the West as a region is a step behind the rest of the country in the organization of communal living. There are a few large cities between Kansas and California whose life is essentially that of New York and Chicago, but they are foreign islands in the western sea. Tens of thousands of square miles in the West are still abandoned to the small town, the ranch, and the wilderness. Many people who inhabit this great territory would resent the implication that they were behind the times; and it is perfectly true, alas, that in the West too there are men who were more likable before they high pressured their lives, and women who were more gentle before they took up contract bridge. But in spite of all this, the tempo of life is slower in the West, as any visitor might see if he himself would shift to a lower gear while passing through.

Most people have tucked away in their memories a picture of fresh and unspoiled countryside, of hills that are not shaved down to golf courses, of farmsteads that are not stores, of byways that do not reek with half-burned gasoline, of nights that are not pierced by the headlights and horns of automobiles. In the West, more easily than anywhere else, one may escape the noise and drive of affairs. Ten miles from the towns, ten miles from the highways lies the wilderness. Westerners grow accustomed to the spell of a snow-peak against the sky, to wind music in the spruce tops, to the exhilaration of just living three thousand feet above the sea. Such is the nature of the major blessings of western life. Most people, perhaps, would find them insufficient to counteract the drawbacks, and perhaps it is just as well. The chief charm of the West is that there one does not have to rub forever against one's fellows and oneself. As long as the West is under-populated it will be the haven for those who find solace against a primitive background, who feel that a man's heart should be large enough to hold a mountain, a forest, and a sunset, and that the environment should be rich enough to supply them.

The tourist who maintains his four hundred miles average from Minneapolis to the Coast will see nothing but sentimentality in these statements. Yet he himself is seeking the very things the Westerner has found. He too will discover them if first he can discover his low gear. Not so long ago a friend of mine drove his Chevrolet car from Portland, Oregon to Missoula, Montana in one long day. It was a record, for no matter what roads he might have taken, he could not have reduced the distance to less than six hundred miles. The region traversed contains some of the most beautiful scenery on the continent: the Columbia River area with its rapids, Dalles, and incomparable waterfalls; one of the largest series of lava flows in the earth's history, with coulees that once carried brave torrents and falls that were higher than Niagara; some of the finest lakes, forests, and mines in the West. Yet my friend saw little but his watch and the road. No business urged him on; in fact he was vacationing, with plenty of time to do as he pleased.

All summer those who live in the West watch the cars dash by. They marvel at the perfection of their mechanism and the short-sightedness of their drivers. It would seem that the ordinary tourist accepts the West merely as a challenge to his daily average. He jumps from one national park to another, seeing little between. And even in the parks he seldom goes where he cannot drive. He sits on the verandah of Many Glacier Hotel and wonders how anyone can be enthusiastic about Glacier Park. He rails at the scarcity of roads and suspects the Great Northern of duping him. Above him rises the most magnificent tangle of mountain ranges in the United States. Trails lead to lakes swarming with gamy trout, to innumerable waterfalls of rare and diverse loveliness, to flower fields of unbelievable beauty, through forests and over rocky divides from which a rough and stony sea reaches to all horizons. But he does not see these things. He is figuring the mileage to Spokane.

Romance aplenty lingers in the West, but it lies just off the beaten paths. Every summer thousands of tourists drive from Yellowstone to Glacier Park. Some stop at Butte to see "the richest hill in the world," but most go through as rapidly as possible. They do not see the site of the first gold discovery in the Northwest, the rare mines of gem sapphires, the place where Chief Joseph of the Nez Perce outwitted some of the best generals in the United States Army. They rush through the valley of the Clark Fork, never dreaming of the geological and historical interests that pave every mile. They bump along the shores of Flathead Lake, one of the largest, deepest, and most beautiful bodies of fresh water in the land, grumbling at the rough roads instead of reveling in a landscape whose equal they may never see. Most of them carry fishing tackle which they plan to assemble when they arrive. Fifty times en route they pass side roads and trails that lead to some of the most superb fishing in America.

There is the town of Dayton, for example, on the west shore of Flathead Lake. Countless automobiles pass through it every season, but few turn up the road that goes to the mountains. At the end of that road lies Lake Mary Ronan, whose waters offer some of the best lake fishing in the West. Silver salmon, rainbow, cutthroat, and eastern brook trout are there in myriads. In late spring and early autumn they will strike the troll before all the line is out. Anyone who keeps a bait moving in the water will catch fish. Sometimes the salmon and the rainbows take the fly, and those who have experienced it know that a five-pound rainbow on a five-ounce rod is alone worth a trip to the West.

When the dog days of full summer are upon the land, good fishing may be had to the east of Flathead Lake. From Big Fork a road climbs east through the exquisite canyon of the lower Swan River, then turns north along the piedmont. Little lakes sprawl over glacial sands, clear as mountain air and alive with black bass. On the hottest day these fish will strike the leech, the plug, and the fly, yielding fine sport in a perfect setting.

The cream of fishing is in the streams. Any stream in the Northwest can furnish almost anyone a few trout, but the best streams lie over the hills away from the highways. The Rockies are divided into parallel ranges which run in a general northwest - southeasterly direction. Between adjacent ranges are broad valleys ordinarily drained by large streams. A few of these valleys still lack roads, and are open only to that caravan of the mountains, the pack train.

The latter part of August is best for packing in the northern Rockies, for then the nights are cold enough to kill the insect pests, but not too cold for sleep; the streams are low and the trout are hungry. Anyone who wets a line in the South Fork of the Flathead River—and anyone driving between Glacier and Yellowstone Parks is in a position to do so—will never regret, and I dare say will never forget the experience. For seventy miles this stream is neither paralleled nor crossed by a road. It flows through a valley thirty miles wide, flanked on the east by the Continental Divide, on the west by the Swan Mountains. A one or two day pack journey from the outposts of civilization on either side brings the traveler to a rugged wilderness of over two thousand square miles, a wilderness that was the same in the days of Lewis and Clark, and no one knows how long before. Here amid glaciated peaks and grassy parks, with only the mountain goat, the elk, and the fool hen to share it, is one of the few remaining Paradises for the lover of the unspoiled.

Toss a grey hackle into the first ripple and watch the big "natives" jump for it. Feel them fight as only fish that live in a torrent of ice water can fight. Fill your creel with three pounders, then fry them over a campfire. Listen to the drowsy talk of the wrangler and then crawl into a sleeping bag under the stars. Do this until your lungs are clean, your muscles hard, your worries gone—and if you are not a Westerner at heart when you finish, you will become one when next winter's memories brew their medicine in you.

Up and down the Rockies adventure lurks in many forms for the traveler whose curiosity is strong enough to lift his foot off the throttle. For those to whom fishing seems too sadistic a diversion, there are other things. Wild life still abounds in the side canyons, and it is thrilling to be able to convince a hunted creature that you are a friend. Marmots, squirrels, deer, and a variety of birds challenge one's finesse at diplomacy. And it is a barren canyon that does not lead to some prospector's dream.

Convenient to the route of the National Parks Highway from Glacier to Yellowstone, the little town of Bearmouth nestles in the valley of Clark Fork. North into the heart of the Garnet Range lies the canyon of Bear Creek. Flanked by walls of multicolored rocks which hold back the rising tiers of pine-topped hills, a wagon road penetrates the gash in the mountains. A little stream winds with difficulty through the jumble of its own rocky accumulations. When spring freshets melt the snow of the higher slopes, the valley annually becomes the channel of a wild river that tears rocks from the mountains and hurtles them to lower levels. But now in mid-summer the stream is quietly expiating its vernal transgressions. Fearlessly the road crosses the watercourse again and again, working its way upward with as much difficulty as the stream works downward.

Here and there the boulders have been more deeply disturbed, and an abandoned, half-wrecked sluice box tells the reason. Presently, where the valley widens, there rises the ghost of a town. The first and largest building is the wreck of a saloon, where men once turned from the discouragement of yellow metal to the solace of red liquor. Here is a house plastered with newspapers telling of events as forgotten as the town that heard of them. Tradition says that more than ten thousand people once lived in this hollow, that ten million dollars in dust and nuggets were taken out of the stream bed. A rusted pan lying on a gravel bar will still bring "colors" for anyone who knows how to operate it.

Farther along, the canyon narrows, the road swings away from the stream in search of more gentle slopes. Where the gravel of the roadbed gives way to corduroyed logs, one had better park the car and walk. These hills and their roads were not made for automobiles. A mile farther, over granite slopes covered with large spruce trees, lies the rolling top of the range and all that is left of the town of Garnet. Long after the placer claims below had been abandoned, mines in the parent veins above continued to grope for treasure. Now they too are abandoned. Water in the deeper workings, litigation, and all the other vampires that suck the vitality out of mines, have done their work. Machinery not yet too shabby to hide its costliness speaks of higher hopes and better days.

There is still a store although customers are few. Its keeper is happy to see you, starts coffee in spite of your protests. He can remember when Garnet could boast a list of a thousand or more voters. One by one, as miners do, they loaded their backs and went down to search for greener pastures. A handful remain, hoping with the prospector's unearthly optimism, that times will improve in Garnet. Soon you will know everyone in town and will have arranged to enter one of the mines. "Yes sir," the caretaker will proudly inform you, "Nancy has produced ten million and there's ten million more in her when they decide to quit fightin' and start minin' again." You will eventually return to your car, your pockets loaded with samples, your heart with regrets at leaving. As you pick your way in second through the tortuous defile, your head will be full of lore that thousands have passed by in their hurry to arrive somewhere not half so interesting. And you will have learned one of the reasons why the Westerner loves his land.

From the southern margin of Colorado a different West stretches its dry fingers upward across Utah and Nevada; outward over New Mexico, Arizona, and California; downward into Mexico. Here the forested slopes and glaciated peaks melt into desert plateaus and basin ranges. It is a land of color and romance, and its heart is New Mexico.

But north or south, few tourists stray from the main highways. Each year thousands of travelers in automobiles and Pullmans follow the Santa Fé roadbed across north-central New Mexico and Arizona. They do not see the Southwest. They do not see the canyon of the Rio Grande cutting across northern New Mexico like a jagged knife gash. They do not see the jumble of lava flows, extinct volcanoes, bad lands, and toothed summits which constitute the most fascinating conglomeration of scenic features in the country.

Until a few years ago the seventy-five miles between Santa Fé and Taos, to say nothing of the surrounding country, was seldom seen by the casual tourist. Today the customary traveler over the Indian Detour sees only the surface. The surface is interesting and beautiful, but the depths are more so. For along the upper Rio Grande the Pueblo Indians live, Indians who were old in art and democracy when the soldiers of Coronado came in 1541. Four centuries of white civilization have destroyed little of their genuineness. The Pueblos still look, talk, think, and feel like Indians. They remain self-supporting and self-respecting under influences which have elsewhere wrecked so many of their blood. Their art, especially their dances, pulsates with primitive vitality and beauty. To know these people and their ways is to enter another world.

Unbelievable events still happen in New Mexico. A mysterious undercurrent of paganism and primitive Christianity flows through the lives of her children. The casual visitor may see a flash of this current when it bursts to the surface in the lurid *matachina* dance at Taos on Christmas Eve. But usually it flows deeply, to be vaguely felt rather than seen, and felt only by those who take time to get close to the heart of this amazing land.

Most mysterious of all is the cult of the penitentes which lingers, despite opposition from the Catholic Church and general public opinion, in some of the remoter villages of southern Colorado and Utah, in eastern Arizona, but especially in northern New Mexico. Tales of the penitentes reach the ears of most travelers in this region, tales that make the hanging of witches seem a gentle sport. Those who stay long enough may witness even now a pageant that almost must be seen to be believed.

The roots of the penitente brotherhood lie deep in time. Long before the Order of Flagellantes appeared in Italy early in the thirteenth century, self-whipping had been practiced by various sects of zealots and fanatics. The underlying philosophy is simple enough. Christ the Saviour was flogged on the way to Calvary. He bore this anguish for us. We should be willing to suffer in the same way so that we may be more worthy of heaven. Grimly the penitente ritual re-enacts the passion of Christ—not as a harmless dramatization but with real suffering. There is reason to believe that men have died on the cross in New Mexico.

Despite great secrecy and the exaggeration of gossip, the corroborated testimony of eye witnesses brings out certain fairly reliable facts. The penitentes have practiced self-whipping for centuries—and still practice it. Some authorities—if there can be authorities on such hidden practices —maintain that no crucifixions have taken place in recent years. Public opposition may well have softened the ceremonies, as it has certainly driven them to the remoter mountain fastnesses. But it has not destroyed them. During Lent, on All Saints' Day, and at funerals, whippings still take place. It has often been alleged that the *cholla* cactus, demon of the plant world, is used to supplement the torments of the whip. In their frenzy both men and women are said to walk barefoot over paths paved with *cholla*, to carry bundles of it upon their backs, and to roll naked upon it, driving hundreds of cruel and poisonous thorns into their flesh.

Such affairs are enacted on occasions of penance which, it would seem, occur not infrequently. Abundant evidence indicates that the major ceremonies transpire during Lent and especially during Holy Week. These ceremonies vary among local groups, but the stories of both eye witnesses and penitentes who have deserted the brotherhood agree in fundamentals.

The early weeks of Lent are devoted to nocturnal prayer in a lonely little windowless *morada*. On Holy Thursday night the door opens, the *pitero* comes forth, making such an air on a reed pipe as to curdle the blood of anyone within hearing of its melancholy wail. Behind him is a man with a lantern, followed by others whose heads are bound in black cloth, naked above the waist, with thin white trousers and bare feet. All these carry fiber whips. The procession, led by the piper, chants dolefully and moves forward, pausing every two steps to allow the whippers to swish the lashes over their shoulders against their naked backs. Blood flows from the wounds and streaks the white trousers. Presently a cross is reached before which the flagellants fall down while the rest sing a hymn. Then painfully, the procession returns to the *morada*.

New members are initiated before the climacteric proceedings of Good Friday. Again in the *morada*, amid chants and high solemnity, the novice pledges himself to obedience, loyalty, and secrecy. By candle-light he receives the official seal—three parallel slashes down the back and across with a piece of broken bottle. The scars of such wounds are still seen by attendants in New Mexican jails, for the brothers are not always so rigid in secular as in sacred affairs.

In the days before a wooden image of the Saviour was used, a live man was chosen for the *Cristo*. Whipping, praying, fasting, and marching proceeded to Good Friday. After early morning whippings and marches, the final procession formed. The frenzied participants, racked by the pain of previous scourging, moved on bleeding feet toward *Calvario*. Women trailed along, as eager to punish themselves as were the men. Half a dozen men may have carried crosses, but the *Cristo* led with the largest, several times heavier than his own body. He stumbled often but somehow carried on for many miles. He never let a groan escape though tears streaked his tortured face. At last the appointed *Calvario* was reached, the *Cristo* was firmly bound to the cross with ropes. The cross was raised and the sermon of the seven last words pronounced. The limbs of the victim slowly turned blue. Before the fatal discoloration reached the heart he was removed to the *morada*. If he did not recover, both he and his family were certain of heaven.

New Mexico is not all horrors. Nor is it, as so many travelers must believe, a long hot drive and a handful of half-spoiled Indians selling souvenirs in Harvey Houses. There is still more beauty and romance off beaten tracks in New Mexico than anywhere else in the country. Each year tourists see Santa Fé, Taos, Puyé, Frijoles, perhaps Acoma and the Carlsbad Caverns as well. Few go beyond these and similar focal points of interest. And few stay long enough both to feel and to see these places. For five months each year the high plateau of northern New Mexico, with its clean air, its varied scenery, its breath-taking sunsets, is a real fairyland for the curious. Ancient cliff dwellings, many of them unexplored, lie deserted in the sunshine. Indian pueblos and Mexican 'dobe villages sleep quietly through the years. It is the land of mañana—lovely, leisurely, mysterious, and old.

To the west lies Arizona. The world has come to it for the supreme grandeur of its sunken river. But the world passes on without noticing many other things of high interest and beauty. Arizona is peppered with national monuments whose very names — Tumacacori, Chiricahua, Casa Grande, Papaga Saguara, Tonto, Montezuma Castle, Walnut Canyon, Petrified Forest, Waupatki, Navajo, Pipe Springs—are alluring.

Just over the line in Utah and Colorado are many more, as well as three national parks: Zion, Bryce Canyon, and Mesa Verde. At these places the desert presents its best offerings, rock formations of weird design and brilliant colors, relics of a great but nearly forgotten chapter in human history. And over all are boundless air and sunshine.

Farther west is California, but not the California of the tourist's dream. From the Colorado River to the Coast Ranges, the Mojave Desert defies both chamber of commerce and subdivider. Generally lower than the high Colorado Plateau of Arizona, the Mojave is hot in summer. When the wind blows, indeed, parts of it can suggest the inside of a blast furnace. Most visitors to the land of sea breezes and orange groves sigh with relief when they have crossed it. Yet the Mojave has compensations for the adventurous—even in summer.

It is June, and I can look down from my campsite on the Funeral Range to the shimmering Hades of Death Valley. The lowest point in the United States is at my feet and over the western horizon is Mt. Whitney, the highest. One of the wildest panoramas in the world lies before me. The valley with its sand dunes and ghosts of forgotten waters is an opalescent gem set in a jumble of colored mountains. Everywhere is the record of violence — outgushings of black lava, gnarled and broken ranges, the tragic human history of the region. Yet all is quiet enough now. The valley inn is closed for the summer, no automobiles crawl over the sandy roads. Last night was full of stars and coolness, and such a calm as civilized man has forgotten. Only a hummingbird reminds me that life exists in the world. He is doing what he can with a desiccated greasewood on the dry wash before the tent.

For days I have been in a desert that nearly everyone avoids at this time of the year. I have thousands of square miles to myself. I am digging a little human history from the débris of dead mining towns, and a little of the remoter history of the earth from the fossil-bearing formations which time and convulsion have not everywhere destroyed. That is my business here. My pleasure is in just being here, nosing through the desert in low. With me are two men who have previously thought me mildly demented for doing such things. But this time I persuaded them to join me, and to their surprise they are having the fun of their lives. For now they are crazy too.

MAZOURKA CANYON

Her enemies have made Mazourka what she is.
The cloudsucking peaks of the Sierra Nevada
steal most of her share of moisture and the
thirsty city of Los Angeles steals much of the
rest. Wind has bruised her gaunt body until today she is as forlorn a piece of wasteland as ever
lost the favor of God and man.

For nearly three decades Mazourka knew little
of rain but the occasional showers that quickly
dried in the dust of her years. Then one day, as
though nature had suddenly revolted against her
own injustice, a black cloud piled up on the Inyo
crestline to the east. It swelled until it broke, and
hurled back to Mazourka in a minute what had
been denied her for a quarter of a century. But

64

alas for such precipitate amends; Mazourka was not ready to accept them. She had no trees to retard the water as it fell, no soil to hold it to her rocky slopes. Rivers rushed through ancient race tracks of the wind.

One small tributary canyon led most of the downpour to the valley below. From its mouth the water stormed unchecked until it reached the bib of rock débris that hangs from the neck of the range at Mazourka's lower end. Ten minutes and the maelstrom might have been a mirage, had not that ten minutes seen more history written into the unhappy annals of Mazourka than the ten years that had gone before.

Geologists stress the slow but insidious workings of natural forces. We arrived at the scene of a desert cloudburst soon after its occurrence, and saw the importance of the occasional violent storm in shaping the destiny of the earth. A jagged gash scarred the mountainside from the place where the water had gathered. At its foot a wall of boulders rose across the canyon floor, and below the valley was either scoured bare or filled with tumbled stone.

Just one of the paradoxes of the desert is that difficulties may arise from the presence no less than from the absence of water. The road we had intended to follow in our car had been carried five miles away and in its place was the jumble of a desert river bed. We sought the advice of John Amick.

Every stretch of wilderness however desolate has some human being to love it. John had loved Mazourka since the day he first searched her rocky slopes for gold. After eighteen years he was still enamored, though his mistress—perhaps because his mistress—had not always yielded him what he sought. Love is seldom easy to explain. John was a prospector and prospectors' feet are restless, but we somehow knew that he would never leave Mazourka.

His shack clung to the side of the alluvial fan at the canyon's mouth. We found him in the doorway, smiling behind his whiskers. After we explained our business there, he said, "Oh, jologists, are you? We've had jologists up here a few times, but most fellers are looking for this." Out came the customary bottle of nuggets, followed on our part by the customary felicitations. Before John arrived in 1913, there was scarcely a gravel bed in the whole range that had not been sifted through the dry washer. But John was observant and industrious, and was continually discovering patches of pay dirt that had escaped his predecessors. And too, he had dug innumerable holes in the "hard rock" for vein gold. Even now at seventy-two, as caretaker of an idle silver mine, he was using his abundant leisure in occupations more typical of gophers than of men.

We hoped to unearth the fossil remains of animals that had lived in the seas whose mud had later dried and buckled into the Inyo Mountains. John had seen shells in the rocks not far away and he was good natured enough to guide us to the exact spot. No evil can come from humoring a fool if all he desires is to dig for worthless specimens. Besides, John was curious enough to be a bit of a fool himself.

He led us south along the corrugated gravels of the piedmont. Half a mile below camp we turned and drove toward the range until the gullies became too deep for our automobile. Girding ourselves with canteens, knapsacks, picks, and chisels, we looked to the mountains on foot. One of John's failures, a hole sixty feet deep, lay by our path. Cloudbursts of a million years pile high their loads of rock débris at the base of desert ranges. Gold, the needle in these lithic haystacks, is heavy and tends to settle on bedrock under the fan deposits. The prospector must often bore through many feet of partly cemented gravels before he reaches dirt that pays. In this case the deep gravels were as devoid of gold as those on top. But that didn't prevent John's digging another hole in another place.

John, in fact, was one of the best diggers in Inyo County. Our path led up a hogback, then turned abruptly along an abandoned wagon road on the side of a ridge at whose inner end a trail took into the mountains. At the end of the trail was a "hardrock" prospect which one of John's city friends recently visited. That gentleman had been born with an inability to walk and had not since entirely repaired his deficiency. The whiskey with which he had filled himself before venturing into the wilderness had not helped. To complete the preparations for misfortune, he was the owner of a Ford, and even when sober was probably imbued with the wonderful confidence of his kind. With more courage than judgment or skill he managed to reach the road that skirted the ridge, and just as he was congratulating himself on outwitting Nature, the road ended. Turning around and backing out were equally impossible. There was but one escape—to make a turning place by digging away the side of the mountain. The dime on which a Ford is supposed to be able to revolve is a large coin when hewn from solid limestone. But John happened along about then, and in two hours the car was facing home.

What is more to the point, John's legs were as good as his arms and shoulders. We were forty years his junior, but we found it necessary at several points to pant our admiration of the view. John was as much goat as gopher, and when he boasted that his lungs and heart were still pretty good, we had no inclination to deny it. For an hour we followed the flaps of his wind-frayed shirt, and arrived at last at the layers with shells protruding from their weathered surfaces.

So many and severe have been the vicissitudes of the rocks in this region that the geologist does not always succeed in deciphering their story. Here by a happy chance were relics of the Devonian seaway that once spread its water where now the desert spreads its rock and sand. We salvaged the shells of many simple creatures who had lived and died a hundred million years ago. Corals, crinoids, and fragments of bivalve animals were abundant. They recalled a day when life in Inyo County was easier than now.

John helped us gather specimens first and listened courteously to our tales of antiquity. He made some sage observations about the "critters" and the manner of their demise. Fossils, though plentiful, were poorly preserved. Search as we might, we found only a few specimens of any scientific value. John thought there were better ones at Barrel Spring.

So it was that we essayed Mazourka in spite of the recent cloudburst. The lower end of the road had completely disappeared, but two miners had since entered the canyon in a car. They must have stranded or arrived, and in either case we wanted to follow them. It was three o'clock when we returned from the fossil hunt and shadow was beginning to darken the western slopes. But we had plenty of water and food, so we decided to enter the inhospitable portals at once.

The less said about that drive the better. It was one of those abysmally foolish enterprises that enthusiasm sometimes dictates to otherwise intelligent people. We followed the tracks of the miners' car as best we could, but lost them wherever the ground had been baked hard. We scraped the bottom of our automobile on bush and boulder until it might well have shrieked with pain and indignation. We filled holes that the flood had left on the canyon floor, and we dug new ones where the slope refused traction. We pushed and profaned and on the whole advanced — about two miles each hour. Presently we reached the dugout that John had offered us for the night.

Desert dugouts are the modern equivalent of the cliff dwelling. They are crude cabins sunk into the side of a hill above reach of cloudburst waters and out of the wind. If used recently enough by the right sort of person a dugout may be warm and agreeable. John had given us keys to all his cabins. He would gladly have given his soul if we could possibly have devised any use for it.

After some debate we decided to press on to Barrel Spring. Either the road had improved or we had grown accustomed to it. By six o'clock we reached our destination, with a little lingering twilight glow to light the camp making. Springs are the miracles of the desert. Their secret reservoirs trap the torrential rains and feed them in slow trickles to the surface. Barrel Spring lies in a gulch half a mile east of Mazourka. Thirsty plants crowd around and form a bit of green jungle on the desert waste, visible for miles. A crude trough of abandoned sluice boxes, stove pipes, and random lumber conveys some of the water to the main valley. We pitched camp near the end of this homespun aqueduct on ground that would have served better for a relief map of the Himalayas than for a bed.

That night one of the miners whose tracks we had followed came from a nearby cabin to visit us. A month before he had been a plumber in Los Angeles. Rather than suffer a wage cut to six dollars a day, he was plying the pick in Mazour-

71

ka's unwilling gravels for nothing. But he had grown the hopes and the whiskers of a true prospector. He had tunneled to bedrock and was expecting the golden harvest any day. When we left, it had not yet arrived, and there was fair probability that his hope would outlast his grubstake.

Morning came bright and brittle after a cool still night. Mt. Whitney and her fellow peaks of the High Sierras caught the pale dawn light and stood like a troop of frozen ghosts against the western sky. A black phoebe was looking toward breakfast from the post of a burro corral not far from the tent door.

Men are less particular about the morning meal when they prepare it themselves in the wilderness than when their wives prepare it for them at home. Neither orange juice nor coffee quite meet the standard of clarity ordinarily required of them, and bacon fried over a gasoline stove frequently goes beyond crispness to cremation. Eggs get half-soled before their tops congeal, and toast—well perhaps it is better to forget the toast. Fortunately the zest of desert mornings makes juices in the mouth that can cope with almost anything.

This morning was so fine, in fact, that we decided on an excursion to "the elbow," where government geologists had reported fossils in abundance. We were on our way before the sun had driven the cool night air off the canyon floor. A mile above camp the valley was so deeply scoured that we had to abandon the car and continue on foot. Another mile and we crossed the delta of boulders that marked the entrance of the cloudburst waters into Mazourka. The road above was untouched, and soon a scattering of piñon trees on the mountain side informed us that we were reaching an elevation of seven thousand feet.

At "the elbow" the canyon walls squeeze the road into a sharp bend. Shattered formations record the travails of birth and existence which mountains as well as men must endure. East of the widest bow in the road lay the formation we sought, a limestone whose frost-riven fragments draped the declivities with graceful talus. Before we had climbed far on these padded slopes, we found the impress of a trilobite, that long dead relative of crab and lobster. For eons the trilobite had ruled the aqueous world, before life had explored the lands, before backboned creatures had risen to supremacy. Man's dominance has been but a moment compared with the long day of the trilobite. Yet the bitter epitaph written by his own remains is all that recalls him now.

Above the talus where the elements had not blasted the rocks from their place in the canyon wall, we found several slabs crowded with the remnants of an ancient society. Many kinds of invertebrate marine animals recalled one of time's lost heydays, when all the water between the poles was warm and friendly to life. Although these fossils marked an epoch of the long Ordovician period and were several million years older than the Devonian fossils in the mountain near John's camp, they were well and abundantly preserved.

Adventure is never far from the naturalist in the field. When life fails to supply it he acquires it vicariously through the book of the earth, the best adventure story ever written. To discover its tales of forgotten times and creatures is to freshen one's own existence. We found not only the record of animals that human eyes had never seen before, but from our position on Mazourka's flank, eight thousand feet above the sea, we also discovered the Sierra Nevada Mountains. Though we had driven their length through the valleys that skirt their roots on either side, we had never really seen them before. From our Inyo eminence the best of this longest unbroken mountain range in the world rose like a mighty wall before us, from the fans of rock waste and blunt-nosed spurs below to the Alpine peaks with their nestling glaciers above. Automobiles moved endlessly over the Owen's Valley road like lines of ants intent upon some insignificant business.

No land is so barren as to escape all proprietary claims. The Forest Service, with very great or very little humor, has extended the boundaries of the Inyo National Forest to include portions of the nearly treeless Inyo Range. But the real owner of Mazourka established title before the coming of the Forest Service. Since a time that no one remembers, the wind has been lord of Mazourka, and this night he came to punish our trespass. He made the tent sway and crouch with his lashings like a cornered beast, until finally, as though sensing a happier prospect, he ran off with the dawn.

The day was still fresh when we climbed the ridge behind camp. Above the spring we found John's fossil beds. After adding several specimens to our collection of Devonian organisms, we continued toward the higher reaches of the range. Presently the Devonian rocks gave place to the older underlying Ordovician formations. Almost at once we were stopped by the faint impression of a tribolite on a chip of limestone. The discovery was unexpected because no identifiable remains had ever been reported from rocks of this particular age in the Inyo Mountains.

The formation was hardly fifty feet thick and it outcropped but a short distance. We searched it literally foot by foot. Several poorly preserved but recognizable fossils surrendered to our picks. Imperfect though most of them were, it was a real joy to collect them because they elucidated one of the least known epochs in the history of the West.

Suddenly we felt the thrill that may come to the collector but once. After gathering many common brachiopods and trilobites, we unearthed a brittle starfish, one of the rarest types of invertebrate fossils ever found. Whereas most other hard-shelled marine animals have recorded their lives more or less fully, the starfishes have moved mysteriously through countless eons to the present. In the formations of all times and places few starfishes have ever been discovered. Though from the oldest system of rocks that ever gave up a fossil starfish, our specimen resembled closely the brittle starfish of modern seas. Two hundred million years have scarcely marked this creature who epitomizes the conservative element in Nature. While other animals were traveling the pathways of evolution, some to glory and others to death, the brittle stars trailed along, escaping distinction and extinction alike.

Before the flush of our excitement subsided we found another specimen, and the morning air was once more set in motion. Gold nuggets could not have pleased us more. Fossil starfishes have little intrinsic worth, little scientific worth, in fact, because they reveal nothing of how starfishes became what they are nor why they defied the challenge of time to become something else. Their chief value is their rarity, but that is enough to warm the heart of any fossil digger.

Not another rock could we jam into the tonneau of our small car. Before leaving we paid our respects to Martin who shared with John an abiding affection for these forsaken hills. He lived in a dugout on the mesa to the west of Mazourka, and each night he could see the sun break and spill its fire on the crags of the High Sierras. A tiny spring allowed him enough surplus water for a small tomato patch. A brush rabbit furnished companionship, a great deposit of gravel insured more work than could be finished in the days that remained. Alone but never lonely, with little that others deem indispensable, Martin was making the desert pay—a bit of gold and infinite content. We turned to the city with a tinge of envy in our hearts.

CONCERNING BAIT

Sooner or later most fishermen discover something in fishing besides fish. Like the fish, the
values of fishing are elusive, sometimes in the
ripples, sometimes in the pools, sometimes even
in an empty creel. But they are always somewhere for the angler with the proper bait.

If a man is destined to become a fisherman, his
first fish will be mounted forever in his memory.
I well recall the event of an August evening that
changed the course of my life. It was dusk over
a mud lake in Illinois. Jolly strains of an accor-
dian floated out of the dark across the lake to
blend in incongruous medley with the croak of
frogs on the nearby shore. Night air came sweet
and heavy off the marshes. Mosquitoes were singing and stinging with joyous abandon.

My companion was arranging the tackle and saying, "This is a swell place. There's a good big juicy one for you." He emphasized the fact by spitting on the worm. "For good luck," he said. "Now fish over by the buoy, and when the cork goes under, jerk hard." Presently I jerked hard and brought up the anchor rope. It was a crucial moment. I was eight years old and could hear a game of tag on shore. Besides, it was growing cold and a mosquito had just drilled me in the neck. I wanted to quit and protested with reason and pathos that I was having a very thin time. May fortune bless my companion wherever he may be! He made me stay and fish. He taught me the old, old password that opens the doors of heaven to fishermen—"Wait!" I waited and soon my first fish was flopping at my feet. From the heights of mature experience I look down upon that fish with a smile. It was distinguished neither in race nor personality. But on that night no one would have dared say so.

We stayed long after dark, long after my friend had had enough, long after the fish had stopped biting. Reluctantly at last I yielded to wisdom. We ran the nose of the skiff aground. Eager to exhibit my prize, I took the bluegill in my hand and jumped for the shore, which I should have reached but for the fateful anchor rope. I slipped and fell—into the boat and despondency at once. For fish slime, gravity, and a last super-piscine wiggle in the bluegill gave him the victory. That night I told the sad old tale. I had become a fisherman.

Fishermen, like other folks, have their own peculiar weaknesses. Among other things they are devoted to the delusion that dead fish grow faster and larger than live ones, that the best fishing is in some other place or at some other time. Perhaps it is just this congenital weakness that glorifies the fishing of boyhood. Yet I do not feel deluded when I recall that in those days we never roamed the arid fields of sophistry. We never troubled our souls in search of the ethical way of luring fish to the bank. We tricked them with worms and feathers alike, with single hooks and triple gangs. We didn't argue morality in the use of baits. Live bait, plug, and fly had no intrinsic worth in our eyes. We judged them fairly through the fish's eyes. We never wasted money on expensive tackle, nor time in untangling it from the bushes. We fished simply. And we were successful, even on those days when we could produce not one sunfish of proof.

No fish was so depraved that we refused him a chance to be caught. We took bullheads from the foul mud sloughs along the big river. We waited placidly amid the rocks and snakes of the wingdams in the gentle hope that suckers would soon be hungry. Buffalo-fish were dedicated to the large task of keeping the river clean, but we were not squeamish. We abandoned them to their business only after learning that nobody would eat them. We even snared the green-fleshed gar-fish, as they lay with their long snouts on the driftwood. We never called pickerel "snakes" and we enjoyed a chub or a catfish as much as a pike or a bass. Anything with a fin and an appetite meant fishing. I should have angled my goldfish out of their globe if they had not been pets.

There is no end to what can be learned about fishing. Boys know this better than their elders and they do not allow methods to harden into convictions. Even Alphonse taught me a thing or two. Alphonse was the chef in a summer hotel. Everybody praised his fried chicken and condemned his fishing. He was addicted to the depraved habit of fishing for that scavenging pig of fresh water, the German carp. He made matters worse by enjoying his vice with all the enthusiasm of a simple heart. He came from a land where carp and carp fishermen were respected, and he could not understand the American sentiment. Unfortunately the poor fellow loved company, but no respectable person would go fishing with him. 81

One day he lured me into his boat with promise of great sport in a very special place. I was prepared for the worst when I saw that raw liver was to be the bait. But I wasn't proud. I had fished for carp myself. We fished all afternoon and caught nothing but carp and dogfish. With each fish Alphonse would exclaim, "Ah, my big beauty, you have come to papa!" And after he had removed the entrails from a dogfish, he would say as he returned the dismembered fish to the water, "There, you rascal, you are now ready for the turtles." Once when the shell of a dogfish swam toward the bottom with the life left in its muscles, Alphonse said a little sadly, "Not another fish in this lake is so strong as a dogfish. See, he still swims when he is dead." His heart was heavy for he hated to admit that not even his culinary skill could make a dogfish fit to eat.

Rowing home, Alphonse praised the carp as the finest of fishes, so big, so game, so delicious. "But," I said, "what will you do with them? Nobody around here will eat them." Alphonse smiled a little smile of professional pride mixed with wickedness. "I fix them;" he said, "tomorrow we all have a lovely bass dinner, and nobody but you and I will know." I was shocked but I kept his secret. For after all Alphonse was in his own way a fisherman. 82

Eddie was different and I learned some more about fishing from him. He had been a pugilist, a maker of bird houses, a dealer in fish, a hotel manager, and I suspected some other things not mentioned. But he liked children and loved fishing. He took me to a little brook where fat young carp lived. For two hours we struggled with adversity, with my ignorace of seining, with Eddy's overfed body, with holes in the net and holes in the stream, and with the refractory spirit of the carp. At last we had a dozen fish of correct size in the bucket. A two mile walk brought us to the lake and a two mile row to the place Eddy had planned to fish. I marveled at his precision. He must have kept a map of the lake bottom in his mind. He had decided that good fishing could be had over a certain sunken reef, and he found the reef marked off, as he had promised, by two lone pickerel weeds whose heads just cleared the surface of the water.

I marveled at his unerring fish sense. He suspended a carp minnow from a float and allowed it to drift about fifty yards from the boat. He fixed a worm on another line, and lowered it over the side. "While we're waiting," he said, "we might as well take a few pumpkin seeds." The boat was soon lively with sunfish. Presently he said, "Now I'll show you something. There should be a few crappies here, but they are deeper than the sunnies." He adjusted the bobber so that his hook hung just over the bottom, and before long he had caught a crappie. It was the most remarkable thing I had ever witnessed.

Soon the line with the carp began to circle the boat. As Eddy had promised, carp minnows apparently were irresistible. With supreme skill he waited until the bass had turned and swallowed the carp, then he set the hook and played the fish through the treacherous invisible hazards of the reef. I was trembling with excitement when he finally hauled the fish over the gunwale. Eddy was as calm as if he had just caught a sunfish, but his face wore a little smile of satisfaction. For it was a large bass and Eddy was human.

I asked him for the honor of stringing the prize. He agreed amiably and I added the bass to the rope already heavy with sunfish and crappies. I placed the handsome string of fish in the water and was fastening one end to the boat when it slipped from my nervous fingers. My heart sank with the fish to the bottom. Eddy just said, "Cheer up, kid," and told me how he had once lost a finer string in the same way. I thought he was the finest fisherman I had ever known. And I still think so.

From one after another I learned the ways and

the joys of fishing. I discovered that frogs could best be taken at night by flashlight along the shore of a lake, that shiners are the surest bait for bass, that fish have better eyes than ears, that the fisherman more often than the wind determines the catch. And I also learned that he is a lucky fisherman who can use a wet fly when trout are not rising to a dry fly, who can fish with a minnow when bass will not take a spinner, who knows how to enjoy the fishing when the fish refuse everything. For the supreme test of a fisherman is not how many fish he has caught, not even how he has caught them, but what he has caught when he has caught no fish.

I suppose it is heresy, but I believe that fish may sometimes spoil the fishing. I remember a crisp November day on a mountain lake in the Rockies. Ice needles had grown into a jagged platform around the shore. We launched a rowboat with difficulty and trolled all day with water freezing on the line. Fishing was never better. Large trout and silver salmon struck the bait before all the line was out. We were too busy to feel the cold and too busy to enjoy the fishing. For after all is said for the fish, there must be some time left for contemplation if the fishing is to be successful. We had no time to watch the muskrats playing on the icy shore. The flame of the tamaracks, the flight of wild ducks, the changing beauty of sky and water did not exist for us. Even the fish lay crushed and unnoticed beneath our feet. We saw and thought nothing but the gory business of capture. We caught the fish but lost the fishing.

Far different was the effect of another day spent on the same lake. It was a summer evening and I was staying at the lodge of a land-locked captain of a Carolina turpentine boat. Tuberculosis had driven the old fellow from the sea to this remote mountain fastness. Fishermen had gathered and talk hummed about the campfire. Each angler defended his favorite lure and boasted of the fish he should catch on the morrow. The captain contributed a few guarded observations. He was dedicated to the happiness of his guests. After the others had retired I asked the captain in confidence just how the fish were biting. "Well," he answered, "right now they are a bit fussy. They may take a 'bass-oreno,' and they may take 'cow-bells,' and they may take a 'daredevlet,' but they probably won't take anything."

He was right. The day was warm and still, and so were the fish. Now, one of the most solemn delusions of fishermen is that nature can be coerced. Yet sweet reasonableness comes at times to us all. The sun was so warm and friendly, the air so good, the world so still. Perhaps I can be forgiven for winding up my tackle and pulling the boat into a reed bed. I stayed there for hours while little waves made soft music on the shore. I know no better way than this of finding the peace that all men seek. I watched a kingfisher snapping up minnows off the shoals, and admired the perfection of his technique. But I did not envy him, for hunger had driven the fun from his fishing. That evening I returned to the lodge fishless but satisfied with my catch.

I often go to see Charlie for Charlie is the spirit of angling incarnate. He lives a simple philosophy. Pleasure is a duty and should be sought, duty is not a pleasure and should be avoided. He had proved the truth of both assumptions during one winter spent in the confinement of a town. That was thirty years ago and time has softened the remorse. His wife left him when Charlie left town and for similar reasons. So now he lives a free life on the shore of a mountain lake far enough from a settlement to feed the solitude hunger that seventy-four years of wilderness have not appeased. Although his daughter seldom visits him, although he has no money except the occasional mite left by a vagrant fisherman for the use of a leaky boat, although life has treated him altogether shabbily, Charlie goes with a smile in his eye. That smile cannot be fired by his bachelor companion, Lew, poor gloomy Lew who "got the catarrh and lost his rememberings." It comes direct from the fisherman's soul of Charlie, for fishing is the grand passion that keeps his spirit as well as his body alive. Three quarters of a century have yielded him this one durable satisfaction, but it is enough. And so with the sun of his life setting, Charlie is gathering tackle and bait for final encounters. Good fishermen know that these will be the best for the finest fishing is just before dark.

A LAKE AND A BOY

It is natural that a boy should love a lake. It is natural that he should love it not because it may be beautiful but simply because it is water. A boy's spirit needs water more than beauty. Perhaps a few drops of the stream wherein life first stirred still flow in him, and breed an ancient longing in his heart.

If a man was once a boy in love with a lake, little is necessary to send him journeying beyond the years. In a glimpse of honeysuckle cascading over a wall in the moonlight, in the distant wail of a locomotive or a snatch of nearly forgotten melody, sometimes in the suggestion of a mere word may lie the magic that makes yesterday of today. The same magic may also make poetry of history and the past can never return to kill the happy illusion.

There was once a certain boy who loved a lake. Because that boy is now a man and the lake a portion of a large city, the two may never meet again in this evolving world. But they often come together as of old in the stabler world of memory. And in that glowing realm, at least, the lake—which is actually only a muddy pond in Illinois—may sparkle like a gem in the slag of the years that have burned away.

Although he did not know it, the lake was his mistress at a time when youth must be a slave to something. The mystery of her depths, the charm of her shores drew his mind and won his affection. She lured him with the innumerable facets of her personality until he came to love her even as did the wild ducks who never left her. And even as they he did not know his heart.

But he knows it now. In retrospect he feels again the caress of her waves when she was happy, their angry beat when she was sad. Once more he seeks the piscine secrets of her dark brown pools, the riddles of her glaciated banks. There clearly is the lone tree still standing guard on the hill; and the woodland paths that lead to the marsh hen's home, to the peach tree lost in the brush. How warm she is in the glow of

August moonlight! He lounges in a boat again just drifting where she cares to take him, no longer longing for answers to youth's unanswerable questions. The waves have washed the questions from his mind.

He sometimes returns to that evening of many years ago when he won the first important victory of his life. He was ten years old and his sole ambition was to catch a pike. He was skittering a frog among the lily pads when suddenly there came a swirl beneath the bait and a tug that nearly jerked the cane pole from his trembling fingers. Anguish nearly ended him while he waited—as he had been told to wait—until the fish had turned and swallowed the bait head on. When he could hold out no longer he struck—and hooked!

The fish made a dive for a clump of pads, but the boy sensed the danger in time. He maneuvered the stubborn creature into deeper water where it rushed from side to side, sometimes lunging under the boat dangerously close to the oars, sometimes driving out like a bullet for the far side of the lake. But eventually it was swimming doggedly by the gunwale until at long last the boy was able to lift it gingerly aboard.

It was the first game fish, the first real triumph of his life. He displayed the prize to anyone who offered the slightest encouragement, and kept it on ice for a week so that no one might be disappointed. His joy would have been complete had not people said, "Now, buddy, you'll have to go out and catch a bass."

He knew nothing of the prejudice against pike, and those who saw his happiness did not enlighten him. Soon, however, he tasted the gall of truth. Returning one evening from a fruitless attempt to duplicate his stellar performance, he saw old Andy, best fisherman on the lake. He called, after the fashion of fishermen, "What luck, Andy?" "Rotten," Andy replied. "Had a couple of strikes but they're bitin' short. Got a couple of snakes here. You can have them if you want 'em."

When the boy saw the "snakes" he experienced his first real grief. Before that time he had twice suffered deeply: once when his dog had been hit by a street car, and once when he had forgotten to feed his pet turtles for a month. But these tragedies were nothing compared with the shock of hearing Andy, his god at the time, call pike "snakes." He couldn't say anything except that he guessed he didn't care for them. He pulled a tearful oar to the shore and refrained from fishing for a week.

But even a pike, if large enough, may gain

for its conqueror a modicum of the world's regard. There was that other summer day when the boy was sixteen. A wind blew gusty and cold from the northeast and the lake was murky after a month of heavy rains. People were huddled around fire-places with the doors of their cottages closed. Fishermen were spinning yarns rather than reels. But the boy had learned to love the lake in all her moods, and fishing even when the fish refused to bite.

He knew that on such days as this, large pike might just possibly be tempted out of their customary lethargy by the flashing blade of a spoon hook. Accordingly he rowed to the windward shore where the water was deep and the weeds sufficiently sparse to permit trolling. After an hour that yielded only numbness to feet and hands, the hook connected with something solid. Now trolling is a form of angling that supplies many a spurious thrill. There are things in a lake besides fish that may entangle a trolling line. Through fifty yards of reeling, the object which had engaged the boy's tackle might well have been a log.

Logs, however, are not given to sudden bursts of animation when drawn close to a fisherman's boat. From the first mad rush which nearly broke the tip off the rod to the last which nearly drew all the line off the reel, the boy was never in doubt as to the nature of the hidden phenomenon. Luck had at last given him the opportunity that all fishermen await. Because he was somehow equal to it, he may perhaps be forgiven for the pride with which he displayed his pike to the admiring crowd that quickly gathered on the hotel porch. It was thirty-nine inches long, and although it has since gained considerably, it weighed all of an honest twelve pounds on the day of its death.

There are times when even the most ardent fisherman must tire of pursuit. On such occasions the boy would sometimes lie in the sunshine, as content as a basking turtle, dreamily aware of lapping waves beneath him and black terns wheeling inquisitively overhead. Sometimes in more active mood he would search the weed-choked bays where water lilies and cat-tails, miracles of the muck, exposed their lavish charms. From these bays the channels that led to other lakes squirmed sluggishly through meadows of hay and swamps of wild water grasses. Life in all its prodigality was there. Minnows frisked over the sedge-guarded shoals; dragon flies buzzed in tandem contentment; cranes stood patiently on one reedy leg attentive for passing prey; great blue herons flapped over their nests in the rice. Drinking in the rich dank odors of the marshland, lazily drifting with the hours, the boy slipped quietly back into an animal's world. And in a world that men have lost he found the happiness that men are seeking.

The lake's domain did not stop at the shore-line, for behind the hotel were the frog meadows. Early in the morning the boy would scrape through the wet grass, eye and arm alert for any luckless amphibian that might jump from cover. Green grass frogs of proper size were a tempta-tion to bass, and no good fisherman was ever without them. Then, too, there was Mr. Benson, the fishing druggist from the city, who could cast a bait farther, more accurately, and more decep-tively than any other fisherman on the lake. He needed many frogs, but the little green devils al-ways outjumped him. Occasionally he allowed the boy to provide bait and motive power at the oars—a very special honor. His invitation always came with the question, "Got any frogs, John?" John always had a sufficient supply; and suffi-cient fortitude as well, though the day were hot and the druggist very fat.

Beyond the meadows lay the woods, and be-yond the woods the rolling farmlands. Every acre held a secret, every secret a challenge. For the boy who was wise in sylvan lore there were many good things in the woods: wild berries, may apples, the nests of birds; there was, indeed, a whole world of adventure stretching all the way to the ice house on the far side of Lake Catherine. And the country roads were only less intriguing than the woodland paths. At the end of one lay the station where the trains came in, and whence the summer pilgrims scattered in creaking carryalls to a score of lakeside resorts. Another wound through fields of corn and alfalfa past an orchard whose apples were the sweetest in the land, and whose owner, by a kind provision of destiny, lived over the hill and out of sight. Yet another one somehow discovered the sleeping village of Centralia and the largest, finest doughnuts this side of Paradise.

Occasionally a chartered launch from across the lake would sidle to the landing, ingorge a motley cargo of sightseers, then churn heavily toward the bridge which marked the channel to Lake Marie. No summer was complete for the boy without at least one such excursion. His lake had many sisters, each with a charm of her own. Traveling from one to another through the choked but navigable waterways by which they joined hands over half a county, the boy thrilled with each new experience. There was excitement in the breezy freshness of Marie, in the queenly expanse of Fox, in the inviting pickerel weeds of Pistakee Bay, in the astounding size and beauty of the lotus which endowed Grass Lake with a unique distinction. But his heart was faithful. When the sun dipped under the green western meadows, he returned to his own lake knowing that she was loveliest of them all.

She held her admirers with charms that never staled, and journeys thus far afield were but periodic diversions. The ramshackle hotel sprawling leisurely under the oaks offered undiscriminative shelter to all. After forty years of service it had become as much a part of the lake as the fish or the loons or the reedy shores. The heat of August dog days might spoil the fishing and dry up the countryside, but it could not keep the little cool breezes from playing on the wide and friendly verandahs. There, when the sun made boating uncomfortable, the lake might yet be enjoyed from a distance. There, too, was rest and play and human companionship. It is the fate of hotels to be much used and little loved, but the Sylvan House was an exception. Even the phoebes nested in her rafters, and the boy would almost rather have seen the water drained from the lake than any harm come to the hotel.

Hotel and lake were, indeed, organically united by the boarded walk connecting the lower verandah with the boat landing, an artery that carried a constant flow of rowers, bathers, strollers, and fishermen. All day long the pier was alive with a varied bustle. Rowboats were continually shoving off, pulling in, chafing at their tethers, or jostling one another when a gasoline launch made its haughty stir among them. Bathers were plopping into the water, shrieking and splashing. A few determined boys were braving heavy odds in the attempt to wheedle sunfish from their homes. Other fishermen were departing for calmer pastures, eventually to return with fish or explanations as the gods might will.

Even at night things happened on the pier. Memory preserves one particular night when a magnificent thought was conceived in Eddy's brain. His idea was none other than to establish a pair of kerosene torches at the end of the pier and to await what their light might lure from the depths. Almost immediately his fondest hopes—and those of the boy who dogged his steps—became reality. A marvelous pageant began to stream through the water. Schools of bluegills that never strayed far from the worm-riddled timbers gathered like submarine moths. The silver sides of crappies flashed golden in the yellow glow. A sword-tipped garfish passed calmly but threateningly by. Presently a snapping turtle as large as a bushel basket came out of the dark and blinked his astonishment. Eddy managed to snare the monster with a hand net, and next day all the guests drank Eddy's health in soup. One by one the lake revealed her deepest mysteries until at last the torches died. But what the boy saw that night remains bright as any day.

Three cow bells nailed to a stick have no great appeal for the eye and even less for the ear, but in producing results they may rank with the pipes of the Hamlin piper. Shaken long and vigorously by Perrin on the verandah of the hotel, they had power to draw men, women, and children from a full mile's radius of woods and water. Fishermen, lovers, and explorers abandoned their happy pursuits to answer the call of the bells, for it was the hoary and irresistible call of the dinner table.

The hotel was, indeed, a mother who guarded well her children. She filled them with simple country food when they were hungry; she sheltered them from the sudden summer storms; she amused them with a multitude of diversions. No matter how large her family grew, no matter how fickle the allegiance of individual members, she never failed to have a smile and a good bed against the night for all.

There were those of her children who could

not suffer a summer to pass without at least one month of family reunion: Mrs. Baker who loved to gossip, and her gawky son who aspired to honors on the tennis court; Mrs. Cling who had lost her beauty and her husband, but not her faith in the peace that a lake may give; Mrs. Thatcher whom a physician had frightened to the brink of the grave, but who still could forget when a fish was jumping at the end of her line. There were young Bates who haunted the dance hall and the bar; Jerry who tinkered endlessly with a reactionary motor boat; Old Grimes who lolled each summer away in anecdotal inebriation. There were the choir boys who descended in droves on the hotel grounds, and whose activities while seldom churchly were never obnoxious. There were Margaret who loved to tend other women's babies and Helen who made full use of her. There were also the casual wayfarers who came for a day from nowhere, and then returned. There was, in a word, the summer hotel's customary agglomeration of humanity, all so different in what they were, so similar in what they sought.

Six days of the week belonged to the lake, but the seventh belonged to the hotel. Each Saturday night she gathered her flock about her for a gusty celebration. Cottagers drifted in from miles around, and by nine o'clock the lobby and the halls and the verandahs were buzzing with expectation. Everyone was dressed within an inch of discomfort. Presently Graffy set aside his cigarette and leaned heavily to his task at the keyboard. The old house trembled as the dancers gained in number and enthusiasm, but it was her hour of triumph and she somehow always held fast.

A poker game plodded stolidly and interminably on in the barroom, oblivious to the curious and the thirsty who were shuffling about. The mayor of Waukegon was making a great pre-election splurge: buying drinks for all, dancing with the old ladies, playing the twenty-five cent slot machine until either his heart or the machine must break. Lawrence was everywhere, spreading cheer with brilliant success among his guests. Even Mrs. Munson was enjoying herself though she only looked on with a mingling of disapproval and interest. Excitement waxed as the evening wore away, radiating from the dance hall and the bar to every far cranny of the building, and to the rustic arbors where adolescents played at ancient games. The moon hung over the water and far away an accordion was singing in the night. Reluctantly at last the revels ebbed as all things must, and the dawn found a sleeping world.   101

And too, as all things must, the lake and those who loved her have known the havoc of the passing years. No more does the old hotel gather her children about her on a Saturday night, no more do music and laughter swell her weather-beaten walls. The city has swallowed all. The hotel and cottages are gone, and in their places are suburban mansions with parked lawns and concrete boat houses. High-powered motor boats crowd the shores where once the kingfisher dove among the reeds, and everywhere the belching of exhausts has routed the peaceful plashing of oars. On the quiet country roads of yesterday, today no walker dares venture. Only the hollow shell of a place remains. Let those who came too late enjoy it as they may. As for the boy who is now a man, there remain the dreams of other days when things were different.